The Teen Witch's Guide to

Spells

Written by Xanna Eve Chown
Illustrated by Luna Valentine

ARCTURUS

SAFETY WARNING

Please consult an adult before lighting candles. Never burn a candle on or near anything that can catch fire. Never leave a candle burning unattended, and keep candles away from children and pets.

ARCTURUS

This edition published in 2022 by Arcturus Publishing Limited
26/27 Bickels Yard, 151–153 Bermondsey Street, London SE1 3HA

Writer: Xanna Eve Chown
Illustrator: Luna Valentine
Designer: Rosie Bellwood
Editor: Donna Gregory

ISBN: 978-1-3988-1520-9
CH010263NT
Supplier 29, Date 0122, Print run 12189

Printed in China

Contents

Introduction

How Spells Work

Spells are a way of drawing on the strength of the unseen forces that exist within the universe, using words, actions, and the power of your mind. There is magic inside everyone just waiting to be unleashed— and this book will show you how.

It is incredibly important to know yourself before you begin spellcasting … What kind of person are you? What are your strengths and weaknesses? When you know and understand yourself, the power of your personality will help you create positive, strong spells. This is because the strongest magic comes from inside you. Spells are the creations of your inner character and most heartfelt wishes.

However, just as we have the power to do good, we also have the power to harm. In harming others, we harm ourselves and warp our own nature. It is important to remember that you must never cast a spell, no matter how good it is, for or on another person unless they have given you their permission.

Any negative spell you cast can come back on you with triple the power. So, if you cast a harmful spell, you will only end up harming yourself.

THE RIGHT INGREDIENTS

Several things have to come together to make a spell
work properly:

1. **The correct spell**
2. **The proper materials and supplies**
3. **The time of the spell**
4. **The state of mind of the spellcaster**
5. **The will of the unseen powers of the universe**

1. THE CORRECT SPELL

Make sure that you have picked the best spell to achieve your
aims. For example, if you want to protect an object, it's essential
to use a spell for protection rather than one for luck.

2. THE PROPER MATERIALS AND SUPPLIES

There are many different oils, candles, and stones that can
be used in spellcasting, and it takes time to build up your
collection. Look in alternative and gift stores for supplies, or
check online stockists for a wider choice. As you become a more
experienced spellcaster, you will collect a variety of tools and
objects that you use in your spellcasting. Keep these objects in a
spell box, wrapped in silk or a fabric that's special to you.

What's in your spell box?

- **Candles**
- **Compass**
- **Crystals**
- **Oil burner and essential oils**
- **Incense and holder**
- **Herbs**
- **Pen and paper**
- **Fabrics in different hues**
- **Ribbons**
- **Scissors**
- **Sewing thread**
- **Small containers for water, herbs, oils, salt, etc.**

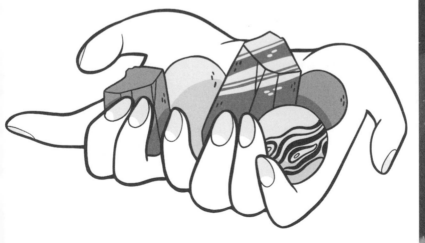

MAGIC WAND

You can cast successful spells without a wand, but using one will add power to your spells and energy. You could buy one from a wand specialist or make one yourself from a piece of wood that you feel a strong connection with. The type of tree the wood comes from has a meaning, too.

The secret meanings of trees

- **Apple—love and healing**
- **Birch—caring and nurturing**
- **Blackthorn—wisdom and protection**
- **Cedar—life**
- **Elder—protection**
- **Elm—love**
- **Fir—birth**
- **Hawthorn—protection and marriage**
- **Hazel—wisdom and communication**
- **Holly—sleep and luck**
- **Ivy—mystery and marriage**
- **Oak—strength and courage**
- **Willow—imagination**
- **Yew—protection and renewal**

MAKE YOUR OWN WAND

1. Cut a stick so that it is the length of your arm from the tip of your middle finger to your elbow.

2. Use sandpaper to rub off the bark, and make sure the wand's ends are not sharp.

3. Leave the wand like this for a natural look, or wind strands of yarn around the handle to decorate it.

4. Before you use it, hold your wand and charge it with magical energy by saying these words:

> Oh, unseen powers
> of the universe,
> I am taking my first
> step along the path
> of knowledge.
> Bless and charge this
> wand with your strength.
> Help me to use it
> wisely and well.

3. THE TIME OF THE SPELL

Many spells need to be cast at a particular time of day. Some need the mystical power of the moon, others require the brighter energies of the sun. Each day of the week has a unique energy and power. For each spell, decide which energy would suit you best, and cast the spell on that day.

- Sunday—ambition, fun, truth, and success
- Monday—emotions, dreams, and imagination
- Tuesday—courage, energy, protection, and confidence
- Wednesday— communication (including phone calls and emails) and information
- Thursday— luck, wealth, and success
- Friday— dating, friendship, and love
- Saturday—tests, patience, and protection

THE MOON

The moon is a vital element of many spells. Look in a diary to find out which days of each month have a full moon. Otherwise, check online—there are several moon phase calculators on the internet.

New moon

The new moon governs new wishes, loves, and projects. It is the best time to cast spells for new beginnings.

Waxing moon

This is when the moon seems to be growing. It is the best time to give extra strength to spells that you have already begun or strengthen something that already exists. It is a good time for luck spells.

Full moon

The full moon gives great magical power and is perfect for healing spells. It is also a good time to charge magical objects with extra energy.

Waning moon

This is the period when the moon seems to be becoming smaller. It is the best time to cast spells that work to lessen or remove something negative.

4. THE STATE OF MIND OF THE SPELLCASTER

To make spells happen, you need materials, the right words, and the correct place and time. All these things are the job of your physical self. But the most important part of making spells happen takes place inside you—and this is the job of your spiritual self. Your mood will have an effect on the spell. It could change the intention of the spell or keep it from working at all. You should be calm and grounded when you are spellcasting.

On days when your physical and spiritual selves are in harmony, you feel happy, confident, and relaxed. But there may be days where you feel sad, worried, and out of balance. Spells can help you with this. As your physical self changes and grows, your spiritual self does, too—but it's up to you how much. Your spiritual self keeps growing until you choose to stop. It is always ready to learn more! The more your spiritual self learns, the better and stronger your spells will be.

You can touch your face and your hands. This is your physical self. Your physical self needs food, water, warmth, shelter, exercise, and play.

You can't touch your ideas and your opinions, your loves and your hopes. This is your spiritual self. Your spiritual self needs guidance, love, support, kindness, forgiveness, and trust.

Both are you, but other people can only see the physical you. They can't see the spiritual you. Both your physical and spiritual selves deserve attention and care.

5. THE WILL OF THE UNSEEN POWERS OF THE UNIVERSE

By casting a spell, you are asking for the unseen powers of the universe to help you achieve your aim. In order for your spell to work, those energies must be willing to assist you. When you call upon unseen energies without focus, your spells are unlikely to work. Improving your ability to focus will help you identify the right spell for a situation.

Focus on ... yourself

To know your true self, you have to be honest with yourself. Face your weaknesses as well as valuing your strengths. Don't forget that sometimes a strength can be a weakness and a weakness can be a strength!

... those around you

Listen to what people say and to what they don't say. Pay attention to their hopes, wishes, fears, and loves. Are their eyes happy or sad? Honest or untruthful? Kind or hurtful? The more you try to understand other people's feelings, the more effective your spells will be.

... the moment

Don't think about what happened yesterday or what will happen tomorrow. To focus on the moment, concentrate on everything you know about this particular moment in time:

1. Where are you?
2. Are you warm or cool?
3. What sounds can you hear?
4. What shapes and hues can you see?
5. What can you smell?

Different Types of Magic

Types of Magic

There are several types of magic, and each works best for certain types of spells. In this book, we will look at:

ELEMENTAL MAGIC

The four elements of air, earth, fire, and water can give extra energy to your spells, because each has its own focus and force.

CANDLE MAGIC

Candles can be used in magic to symbolize your intentions. Burn one while you are meditating to strengthen the success of your spell.

CRYSTAL MAGIC

Crystals store energy and have their own vibrations. For these reasons, they are often used in healing spells.

BINDING MAGIC

A rope, string, or ribbon can represent the intention of
your spell. Tying knots in them helps to declare your
goal, bind your spell, and keep it working.

TALISMANS

These are charms or amulets that
are given power through the
casting of a spell, and they are
usually made to bring good
luck or protection.

NATURAL MAGIC

Flowers, leaves, herbs, and oils are
often used in pouches or bags
to make talismans. There are many
different kinds available for
different purposes.

ELEMENTAL MAGIC

For a spellcaster, the four elements are earth, air, fire, and water. These represent the energies that make up everything in the world.

EARTH

Love, luck, and money spells use earth energy.

Hues: Green and brown
Direction: North
Tools: Stones, salt, bowl of soil

AIR

Spells to do with the mind—for example, to improve concentration—use air energy.

Hues: Purple and yellow
Direction: East
Tools: Incense, wand, visualization

FIRE

Spells for success, creativity, and strength use fire energy.

Hues: Red and gold
Direction: South
Tools: Candle, lamp, burning herbs

WATER

Healing and cleansing spells use water energy.

Hues: Blue and white
Direction: West
Tools: Bowl of water, mirror, goblet

CANDLE MAGIC

Candle magic calls on the element of fire to energize your spells. You can use a candle to focus your intention and release that energy into the world when you burn it.

There are lots of different kinds of candles you can buy, and the ones you need will vary from spell to spell. Spell candles are often very small—about the size of the ones you get on a birthday cake—and need a holder to keep them standing up. Tea lights are useful as they can be found in all the shades of the rainbow and have a foil holder to contain the wax. (This holder will get very hot, so make sure it is on a fireproof plate when in use.)

Which candle to choose?

- White—purity, truth-seeking, and peace
- Purple—hidden truths and psychic powers
- Blue—wisdom and protection
- Brown—friendship and support
- Orange—fairness and justice
- Pink—romance and caring
- Green—healing and growth
- Red—passion and strength
- Gold—success and happiness
- Yellow—imagination and intelligence
- Silver—dreams and intuition

CRYSTAL MAGIC

Crystals and stones have been used for thousands of years for magical and medicinal purposes. Choose four stones that represent the elements and keep them in a special bag, or place them in your spellcasting area. You will feel more of a natural connection to certain crystals. Let your instinct draw you to the crystals that are meant for you. Choose:

- A clear or yellow stone for air
- A red, orange, or black stone for fire
- A white, blue, or turquoise stone for water
- A green or brown stone for earth

Crystal powers

- **Agate**—grounding, success, and good fortune
- **Aventurine**—creativity, health, and good luck
- **Carnelian**—peace, bravery, and safe travels
- **Citrine**—spiritual wisdom, courage, and self-confidence
- **Clear quartz**—spirituality, love, and healing
- **Hematite**—grounding, spiritual development, and overcoming nervousness
- **Jade**—health, healing, and perfection
- **Malachite**—sleep and the heart's desire
- **Onyx**—meditation, protection, and dispels nightmares
- **Red Jasper**—grounding, inspires friendship, and defends the home
- **Rose quartz**—love, appreciation, and peace of mind
- **Snowflake obsidian**—protection, ends difficult times, and overcomes obstacles
- **Tiger's eye**—protection and looking beneath the surface
- **Turquoise**—health, friendship, and happiness

BINDING MAGIC

Knot magic involves tying or untying knots to bind or release a spell. You can make a knot in anything—ribbon, thread, string—even a scarf or a sock! You put your intention into the knot by reciting a spell or visualizing an outcome as you tie it. While it is tied, the knot contains the magic spell. When the knot is untied or cut, the magic is released back into the universe.

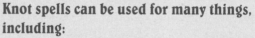

Knot spells can be used for many things, including:

- **Arguments**—The knot binds the anger, allowing you the chance to make friends again.
- **Friendship**—The knot binds you together.
- **Luck**—The knot draws the luck in and binds it to you.
- **Healing**—The knot binds the pain to allow the patient to get some rest.
- **Weather**—The knot binds the stormy weather and keeps it away for a little while.

A magic knot—or "witches' knot"—is a symbol of protection. The line that makes up the four loops must be drawn without taking the pen off the paper.

MAGIC TALISMANS

A talisman is an object that has been charged with magic. It can protect, heal, or bring luck, and it is usually something small that you can wear or carry with you. Every time you wear or carry it, it amplifies your power. A common talisman is a metal circle, engraved with magic symbols and worn around the neck. However, it can be anything that holds personal meaning.

Talismans have been used since the times of ancient Egypt. Popular symbols were the ankh, the Eye of Horus, and the scarab beetle. These symbolize life, protection, and transformation.

Examples of talismans:

- A stone you found in a special place
- An object given to you by a loved one
- A pendant, ring, or bracelet
- A lucky coin
- A symbol drawn on paper
- A small figurine or toy
- A meaningful photograph
- A candle
- A runestone
- A well-loved book

NATURAL MAGIC

Spellcasting works best when natural ingredients are used. This is because these ingredients are part of the world in the same way that we are, and so our energies are more closely in tune.

Herbs and flowers

- For home spells—chamomile, lavender, aloe, gardenia, black pepper, nettle
- For friendship spells—lemon, rose, passionflower
- For luck spells—apple, hazel, holly, ivy, mint, rowan
- For love spells—basil, ginger, honeysuckle, jasmine, mistletoe

Essential oils

- For spells to bring energy—lemon, basil, peppermint
- For spells to bring harmony—myrrh, neroli, sandalwood
- For spells to bring love—cinnamon, ylang-ylang, clary sage
- For spells to bring wisdom—frankincense, nutmeg, rosemary

Smudge sticks

A smudge stick is a bundle of dried herbs that is burned to clear the energy and air of a space, object, or person with its smoke. The main herb used is sage, because it has healing and cleansing powers.

Preparing for Spellcasting

Your Spellcasting Space

You will need a special space in which to carry out your spellcasting. Choose a quiet, safe place where you will not be disturbed and where you are allowed to burn candles. Your bedroom is probably the best place to choose.

Before spellcasting:

- Turn off your phone.
- Tidy any clutter.
- Clear your mind of worries about homework or chores.
- Avoid objects that contain LED displays, such as digital radio alarm clocks.
- Take off your watch or fitness tracker.

Remember, you are stepping aside from the ordinary world. Set aside a special outfit that you will only wear during spellcasting. Many spellcasters choose to wear white, but you should wear something that works with your energy. Above all, you should feel comfortable in it. If you wish, you can decorate your clothing with symbols that are meaningful to you.

Prepare your spellcasting space before you begin each spell by following the steps below:

1. Brush or vacuum the area, focusing on cleansing and purity.
2. Once it is clean and tidy, sprinkle a few drops of water over the space.
3. Cover the area with a beautiful cloth, and meditate on the spells you will perform in the future.

USE YOUR SENSES

Take a moment to think about the area around your spellcasting space. Is it messy, with clothes and books lying around everywhere? This could result in messy energies affecting your spell. Think about your senses as you look around.

Sight

Your spellcasting space should be harmonious and peaceful. The energies of your surroundings affect your mood—and therefore your spell. Make sure that your space is clean and tidy and makes you feel content.

Smell

The sense of smell is extremely powerful and is strongly connected with memory. If there are any negative aromas in your room, cleanse the area by burning incense or essential oils.

Taste

There should be no half-eaten foods around your spellcasting space, and you should avoid eating anything strong-tasting before the spell. The taste in your mouth should be pleasant, and you should not feel hungry or thirsty.

Touch

Harsh fabrics, unpleasant textures, and dusty or sticky surfaces will clog energy and make it more difficult for your spells to work.

Hearing

If you live with other people or near a busy road, there may be noises that disturb you. This is why meditation is important. If you focus on the present, other sounds will fade into the background.

THE RULES OF ENCHANTMENT

Before you try your first spell, you must be sure that you understand (and mean) every word of the spellcaster's promise. Find a quiet, safe place where you won't be interrupted. Look into your eyes in a mirror as you speak the words of the promise.

The spellcaster's promise

I ask my physical and spiritual selves
to exist in harmony.
I ask for the strength and wisdom
to keep them balanced.
I will not neglect the needs of my body
for the sake of my spirit.
I will not neglect the needs of my spirit
for the sake of my body.
I will work hard to help my spiritual self grow.

I ask for the wisdom to listen to the needs of others.
I ask that my understanding will grow all my life.

I will not cast a spell to harm another.
I will not cast a spell to make another
behave, feel, or think in any way against their will.
I will not cast a spell for or on anyone else, unless they
know about it and have asked for or allowed it.
I will never cast a spell when I am angry or unforgiving.

I will develop a calm state of mind
in which to cast spells.
I will train my mind to think of all people
in the light of love and forgiveness.

This is my promise.

PREPARING YOURSELF

When you cast a spell, you should be in as pure a state as possible.
This means cleansing both your energy and your body.
This purifying bath will clean both your spiritual self
and your physical self.

You will need:

- White candle
- Second candle in a brighter shade
- Two drops rosemary oil, three drops lavender oil, and one drop lemon oil, blended together
- Oil burner
- Glass of mineral water

What do to:

1. Burn the oil blend in an oil burner.

2. Run your bath, focusing on the water and thinking about the intention of the spell.

3. Light the candles and place them in safe places around the bathtub.

4. Get into your bath and relax.

5. Halfway through your bath, drink the glass of water. Imagine it cleansing your body as you drink it.

6. Keeping your mind focused on your intention, snuff out the candles, then get out of the bathtub.

7. Dry yourself with a clean, white towel, and then prepare for spellcasting.

> Another way of cleansing is to shower, because it keeps the water flowing. As you shower, make a picture in your mind's eye of all impurities being washed away.

Make Time for Meditation

A relaxing meditation will put you in a good frame of mind in which to cast a spell. It will also help you with challenges you might be facing in life. If you have never meditated before, this is a good basic meditation to start with.

SIMPLE MEDITATION

1. Go outside and find a quiet, safe place where you can sit down.

2. Close your eyes and think about your sense of touch. How does the breeze feel on your face? Is your skin being warmed by the sun or made wet from the rain?

3. Now listen to the sounds around you. Focus on one at a time, concentrating on natural sounds such as birdsong, rather than cars.

4. Next, use your sense of smell. Again, try and focus on natural smells, such as flowers and earth.

5. Finally, be aware of all three senses at once. Put your senses in the middle of your mind, and let everything else flow away.

GROUNDING YOURSELF

It can be dangerous to perform a spell without first having grounded yourself. Grounding yourself is a way of keeping you in touch with reality, and it protects you from dangerous energies. You can learn many ways to ground yourself, but here is a simple routine to get you started.

1. Sit still with both feet on the floor, parallel and about 20 cm (8 in.) apart.

2. Imagine that there are roots coming out of your feet and growing downward, deep into the earth.

3. Visualize yourself connecting with the earth, then speak these words:

> **I value and respect the unseen powers of the universe.**
> **Each day, I try and understand them more clearly.**
> **I ask for strength and support.**
> **I ask for the wisdom to understand and the strength to forgive.**
>
> **I will only ask the energies of the universe to work for good.**
> **I do not wish to harm any living thing.**
>
> **Those powers belong to the universe,**
> **And I am part of the universe.**
> **I am part of the strength and the power,**
> **But the strength and the power do not belong to me.**
> **I belong to the universe.**
> **I am part of the universe.**

STARTING AND ENDING YOUR SPELLCASTING

Even if your spell does not use a candle, you can increase the power of a spell by charging a candle with magical energy before you start. Sit in a quiet place, and hold an unlit candle with both hands. Imagine the energy of the universe flowing into your body, mixing with your own and flowing through your hands into the candle. Say: "I charge this candle with energy and power. May it burn with a strong flame and work for good." Then light the candle, letting it burn as you cast your spell.

Candle signs

- Flame burns evenly—the spell will succeed.
- Flame is weak—someone is trying to block your spell.
- Flame burns well, then gives off smoke—the spell will work well at first, but other problems might arise.
- Flame gives off smoke, then burns well—things will seem difficult at first but will improve.
- Flame goes out before the spell is complete— you are not using the right spell.

It is just as important to end your spells correctly as it is to begin them correctly. You have been acting as a channel for unseen energies. Those energies have to return to their natural home. Always take a moment to visualize them passing through you and returning to where they belong at the end of the spell.

Spells for You

Sweet Dreams

To achieve a good night's sleep, you need to be relaxed. If your thoughts are whirling, you will have a restless night full of disturbing dreams. This is a spell to perform in your bedroom when you are ready for bed. Before starting, sit quietly on the floor with your eyes shut. Visualize a mirror on the outside of your closed door. Now picture the mirror reflecting all negative energy away from you as you sleep. Take several slow, deep breaths, then open your eyes.

You will need:

- Sprig of holly
- Piece of malachite
- Pen and paper

A SPELL TO GIVE YOU A GOOD NIGHT'S SLEEP

1. Place the holly at the bottom of your window, then sit on your bed, holding the piece of malachite.

2. Write down all the things that are upsetting you at the moment.

3. Pass the malachite over the bed three times in a figure-eight pattern. This is the sign of eternity.

4. Wrap the paper around the malachite, and place it under your pillow, saying this incantation:

> **Take away all cares and tears,**
> **Slumber should be free from fears.**
> **Holly and crystal grant good sleep,**
> **With no more need for counting sheep.**

5. Go to sleep. In the morning, hold the paper under running water, tear it up into small pieces, then recycle it. Place the malachite below your window, next to the holly.

HEALTH AND HAPPINESS

This is a spell to perform at the time of a new moon. Before you start, take a moment to sit quietly in meditation and focus your energy. Start by visualizing clear, flowing water, then picture healthy vegetables growing in the ground and fruit growing on trees. Now think about your body running, jumping, cartwheeling, and stretching. Remind yourself that it is the only body you have, and you must treat it with respect.

You will need:

- 3 dried bay leaves
- Pen and paper

A SPELL TO ENCOURAGE GOOD HEALTH

1. Write your wish for good health on the paper.

2. Fold the paper into thirds and put the bay leaves inside it.

3. Visualize the things that you will need to do to enable the wish to come true.

4. Fold the paper into thirds again the other way, then speak the words of the incantation below.

5. Hide the folded paper in a safe, dark place.

INCANTATION

Grant me water, clear and sweet.
Grant me wholesome food to eat.
Grant me wisdom from above.
My body needs respect and love.

Dance Magic

This is a spell that can only be performed by the spellcaster, on the spellcaster! It is a fun and energetic spell, full of noise and self-encouragement. Perform this spell in the daylight, but choose a time and place where no one will interrupt you. You may feel a little embarrassed at first, but why worry? No one is watching! Let your fears go, and imagine the music carrying them away with its rhythm.

You will need:

- Bell, rattle, or tambourine
- Upbeat music

A SPELL TO GIVE YOU CONFIDENCE

1. Choose one of the affirmations below.

2. Play your music until you can feel the beat in your body, like a heartbeat.

3. Dance around the room with your instrument, making as much noise as you can.

4. As you dance, call out your affirmation in a positive voice.

5. Repeat the affirmation nine times as you dance.

6. Repeat the spell once a week, and watch your confidence soar!

AFFIRMATIONS

- **I have the confidence to do anything.**
- **I am sure of myself.**
- **I can solve any problem.**
- **I have faith in myself.**

A Bag of Bravery

When you wish to be more assertive with friends or family, carrying a charm bag in your pocket as a talisman will lend you great power.

You will need:

- Square of yellow fabric
- Yellow ribbon
- Two pinches of ground nutmeg
- Two drops of pine essential oil
- One pinch of dried lavender

Learning to be a spellcaster will help you feel more confident and assertive. To be a good spellcaster, it is vital to truly know yourself. The more you know your own mind, the easier it is to say what you think to others.

A SPELL TO BE MORE ASSERTIVE

1. Lay out the fabric, then place the nutmeg and lavender in the middle. Add two drops of pine oil.

2. Bring the corners toward the middle to make a pouch, and tie them together with the ribbon. Use a double knot and then a double bow, and speak the incantation as you tie.

3. Keep the bag in your pocket. Focus your mind on it to feel a surge of power and energy.

4. Every day for seven days, approach one new situation where you need to be assertive, drawing strength from the charm bag.

5. At the end of seven days, assess whether you still need the bag. If not, scatter the contents outside to all four compass points.

INCANTATION
Double knots, be strong and hold.
Double bows, be brave and bold.
Charge this charm with strength and fire,
For just as long as I require.

CLEAR THINKING

This spell will help you feel cool, calm, and collected. Before you start, think about a time when you lost your temper. Identify the words or actions that made you angry. Next, think of a time when you felt peaceful, and visualize how good it felt. This state of mind is your goal.

You will need:

- Cup
- Mint tea
- Honey
- Dark stone or pebble
- Plastic bowl of water

INCANTATION

**I: Anger, temper, pass on through.
I have power over you.
II: Mint to cool and clear my mind.
Honey sweet to cheer and bind.
III: With this stone, my anger's gone.
Waters flow, and let it go.**

A SPELL TO CONTROL YOUR TEMPER

1. Prepare a cup of mint tea, then start to breathe in the sweet aroma.

2. Visualize a circle of light around yourself. Hold the dark stone over your stomach.

3. Speak Part I of the incantation, concentrating on sending your negative energy into the stone.

4. Still holding the stone, carefully stir two spoonfuls of honey into the mint tea and say Part II.

5. Next, drink the tea, and visualize it flushing the last of your anger out into the stone.

6. Gently throw the stone into the bowl, swirling the water around as you speak Part III.

7. To complete the spell, bury the stone outside, pouring the water from the bowl on top of it.

Spells for Home

Safe and Sound

Use this spell to give extra protection to your house or to increase your own sense of safety when you are at home. Before you start, ground yourself and use a meditation to achieve a peaceful state of mind. Visualize the things that make your home feel happy and secure. You should perform this spell in your house, preferably in the morning.

You will need:

- Old key (look in old drawers, junk shops, or antique markets)
- Red ribbon

INCANTATION

Lock in love and happy life.
Lock out danger, hate, and strife.
Lock in safety, lock in trust.
Turn all evil thoughts to dust.

A SPELL TO PROTECT YOUR HOME

1. Pick up the key in your right hand, and hold the red ribbon in your left hand.

2. Tap the door of the room you are in three times, saying the incantation aloud.

3. Move on to the next door. Repeat until you have visited every door in your house.

4. String the key on to the ribbon, then tie up the ribbon with a double bow.

5. Place the key in a drawer in your kitchen (the heart of the house).

KEEP THE PEACE

Before you can restore a sense of peace to a place, you must first understand what has caused the problem. If there has been an argument, talk to the people involved. If a visitor to the house is causing problems, focus on the reasons why that might be. In the case of accidents or breakages, think about how serious the damage is and how it will be fixed. Remain positive. This is a spell that can be done at any time, when everyone is at home.

You will need:

- Enough salt to fit into the cupped palm of your hand
- Fireplace (or a white candle if you have no fireplace)

INCANTATION

Unseen powers, wisdom lend.
The time has come to build and mend.
Focus every thought and power,
To heal and soothe this very hour.

A SPELL TO RESTORE PEACE IN YOUR HOUSE

1. Gaze into the flames of the fire (or into a candle flame), and think about what has broken the peace. Focus on the events—what led to this situation?

2. Think about the emotions that are bringing a bad atmosphere to the house. (Anger? Fear? Hurt?)

3. Speak Part I of the incantation.

4. Think about the solution to the problem. What is needed to restore peace?

5. Throw the salt on the fire, and speak Part II of the incantation. If you have no fire, carefully sprinkle the salt around the candle, then snuff it out.

BRIGHT BLESSINGS

The more sensitive you are, the more you will be affected by the energies in a house. For this reason, it is important to wash a new home clean of any old energies or events that could leave a bad impression. Your new home will then be cleansed and ready for a fresh start. You should perform this spell on the first night you spend in a new house.

You will need:

- Clean jar with a lid
- White sage incense stick
- Salt

INCANTATION
**Unseen powers, cleanse and clear,
Any pain that once was here.
Make this home feel fresh and new,
Inside out and through and through.**

A SPELL TO BLESS A NEW HOME

1. Put a few pinches of salt in the jar, and light the incense stick.

2. Visit each room in the house, carrying the jar in one hand and the incense in the other.

3. In each room:
   - Make a picture in your mind of the salt soaking up all negative energies.
   - Waft the incense smoke around the room, particularly the doors and windows.
   - Speak the incantation aloud.

Spells for School

SUCCESS STORY

This is a useful spell if you have to take any kind of test or face a difficult challenge. You'll probably find that you need it most often at school, but you can apply it to any situation. Most spells require a certain amount of visualization, but it's especially important in this one. Your visualization of success is the channel through which the unseen forces of the universe will pass to help you. Cast this spell during the time of a waxing moon, outdoors on a sunny day.

You will need:

- Gold fabric
- Green thread
- Marigold petals
- One teaspoon of ground cinnamon
- One teaspoon of ground ginger
- One teaspoon of lemon peel
- Three drops bergamot oil
- A small silver coin

INCANTATION

Great sun, the source of strength and power,
Infuse this charm within an hour.
Success as bright as sunny rays,
Triumph crown my nights and days!

A SPELL TO BRING SUCCESS

1. Visualize the success you require. For example, if you want to win a sporting event, visualize yourself holding up the trophy.

2. Mix all the ingredients together in a bowl. Then fill the pouch and tie the top with the green thread.

3. Hold the pouch up to the sun, and speak the incantation.

4. Lay your pouch in the sun to charge it. This should dry out the oil.

5. Keep it with you at all times. Whenever you can, hold it up to the sun and visualize your success.

Brain Booster

Everyone goes through times when a subject or a project just seems too difficult, and you don't know where to start. You might feel like giving up—but don't! This spell will not turn you into a genius overnight, but it will make it easier for you to learn and understand things more quickly. You should perform this spell at night, during a waxing moon.

You will need:

- Gold tea light
- Orange tea light
- Yellow tea light
- Cinnamon incense
- Mint
- Rosemary
- Small bowl
- Three drops vanilla extract
- Oil of your own choosing

INCANTATION

I ask the unseen powers and forces of the universe to channel power into me.
Help me learn and absorb information, as I absorb the unseen power.
May I reach my full potential in everything I do.

A SPELL TO IMPROVE YOUR BRAIN POWER

1. Put the candles in a line, with the gold candle in the middle, and light the incense.

2. Mix the mint, rosemary, oil, and vanilla extract together in a small bowl.

3. Use your finger to rub a little of the mixture around the middle of the candle.

4. Strike a match above the yellow candle, focusing on the unseen powers you are calling upon. Speak the first line of the incantation, and light the yellow candle.

5. Strike a second match above the orange candle, focusing on your ability to channel and absorb. Speak the second line of the incantation, and light the orange candle.

6. Strike a third match above the gold candle, focusing on your goal of brain power and intelligence. Speak the last line of the incantation, and light the gold candle.

7. Allow the candles to burn out.

Memory Magic

Do you ever find your mind wandering in class? Is it sometimes difficult to remember everything you were taught? This spell will help you free your mind from distractions and focus on your studies. It's especially helpful before tests and exams.

You will need:

- Large pinch of dried rosemary
- Large pinch of dried basil
- Small pinch of caraway seeds
- Large pinch of chopped, dried lemon peel
- Square of purple fabric
- Silver thread

INCANTATION

I call on the energies and power of words
To help me focus on the wisdom they hold.
Let me use language with thought and skill.
Remove confusion and make me bold.

A SPELL TO IMPROVE YOUR MEMORY AND POWERS OF CONCENTRATION

1. Mix the herbs and the lemon peel together in a bowl while chanting the incantation.

2. Lay out the fabric, then place the mixture in the middle.

3. Bring the corners toward the middle. Tie them together with the thread to make a small pouch.

4. Carry the bag with you at all times, and keep it in sight whenever you are working.

5. Whenever you need to concentrate, focus on the sachet.

6. Refresh your lucky bag every two weeks.

Attitude Adjuster

It's hard to keep a positive mental attitude, especially if you're finding school tough or having problems with friends or family. However, these are the times when a positive mental attitude is most important. This spell can only work if you are open to the positive possibilities—and that means expecting the best, planning for success, and believing in yourself.

INCANTATION

I will stay above the line.
Mistakes I make, I claim as mine.
I take control of my own life
And fearless face both joy and strife.

You will need:

- Paper and pen
- Yellow tea light candle
- Agate

A SPELL TO IMPROVE YOUR ATTITUDE

1. Draw a horizontal line halfway down the piece of paper. Above the line write: Seize, Truth, Accept, Respond. Below the line write: Defend, Refuse, Anger, Guilt.

2. Place the agate beside the candle and light it.

3. Speak the incantation, and then pick up the agate and trace a figure eight over the paper with it.

4. Hold the agate to your forehead, and visualize all your negative thoughts flowing out through the crystal and disappearing.

5. Snuff out the candle, and stick the piece of paper to a mirror where you will see it every day.

Remember, as long as you stay with the "S-T-A-R" qualities above the line, the unseen forces of the universe will help you to stay positive. If you don't accept responsibility, you'll be filled with negative emotions. (A total "D-R-A-G!")

Calm Charm

Your mood can be affected by all kinds of unpredictable things—including the weather, the moods of others, and your health. However, there are times when you know that you need to be calm and focused. This spell will help you keep your energies in balance—and if your energies are balanced, you will feel better. It is good to cast this spell outside, in the light of day.

You will need:

- Bowl of water
- Single white flower without a stalk
- Green tea light candle
- Yellow tea light candle
- Jasmine incense

INCANTATION
Earth and light be mixed in me,
Fresh and calm as summer sea.
Keep me focused deep within,
Let a brand new day begin.

A SPELL TO KEEP YOU CALM

1. Float the white flower in the bowl of water, meditating on its beauty.

2. Light the candles and incense, and think about the freshness and strength of nature.

3. Stand with your feet about 20 cm (8 in.) apart, and think about your connection with the earth on which you are standing. Imagine energy rising up into you from the earth through your feet.

4. Reach your arms upward, and imagine energy moving down through your fingertips from the light.

5. Visualize the energies mingling inside you, healing and balancing.

6. Say the incantation, and let the candles burn out.

7. Finish the spell by sitting quietly and imagining the calming energy in the middle of your body.

Gossip Begone!

When someone is gossiping about you, it can be very upsetting. But the code of sorcery does not allow you to cast a spell in anger. Think about why this person is spreading gossip. Are they unhappy about something and trying to distract themselves? Have you upset them by accident, so they want revenge? When you understand the reason for their actions, it will become easier to forgive them. When you are calm and have truly forgiven the person, you may cast the spell.

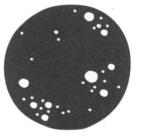

You will need:

- Piece of paper that the gossip has touched
- Box with a lid
- White tea lights

INCANTATION

Unseen powers, hear me say:
Gossip and anger take away.
Open up a path of peace
That love may win and
malice cease.

A SPELL TO STOP GOSSIP

1. Put the paper in the box, and close it tightly.

2. Hold the box with both hands, and speak the words of the incantation.

3. Place the box in your spellcasting space, and surround it with white tea lights. Light them and meditate as they burn out. Think about the person and why they have been gossiping. Be honest!

4. When the gossiping has stopped, remove the paper from the box, and hold it under flowing water.

5. Finally, tear the paper into tiny pieces and then recycle it.

Finding Friends

Attracting friends is like turning on a light inside the house and letting them know that you would like a visitor. After you have performed this spell, you will meet people who are potential friends. However, you need to be able to recognize them—and that means paying attention to those around you. Switch on your light! This spell is most powerful if you cast it during a waxing moon.

You will need:

- Three brown or bronze candles
- Pen and paper
- Gold thread

INCANTATION

In my heart, an empty space.
Bring a friend to fill that place.
Shine on me like glittering sun.
Double joy and double fun.

A SPELL TO MEET NEW FRIENDS

1. Light the candles.

2. Write on the paper three qualities that you would like a friend to have, and say each one aloud.

3. Fold the paper in half, and hold it high above the candles. (Make sure it doesn't burn!) Repeat the three words, speaking them at the candle flames. The flame should flicker but not go out.

4. Speak the incantation.

5. Snuff out the candles, then wrap the paper around them, tying the bundle with the gold thread.

6. Keep the candles in a safe, dark place.

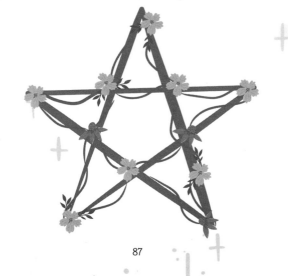

Positive Enchantment

This spell sends positive energy and encouragement to another person. It is a gift that you give, and your reward will be to see your friend feeling better. Cast this spell in a space that is special to you and your friend at sunset, during a waxing moon.

You will need:

- Jade crystal
- Frankincense oil
- Oil burner

A SPELL TO SEND POSITIVE ENERGY

1. Pour some oil into the burner, then light it.

2. Carefully pass the crystal through the fumes from the burner three times.

3. Face the direction where your friend is, and say the incantation.

4. Visualize a shell of energy building up around the crystal. Then place it beside your bed, and picture the energy being directed toward your friend.

5. Imagine the energy reaching your friend and surrounding them with a light of confidence.

6. Next morning, wash the crystal under running water and then give it to your friend.

INCANTATION
Unseen forces, brave and bright,
Send [friend's name] help and
strength tonight.
Give them the self-belief of youth,
Crowned with success and
throned in truth.

PEOPLE POWER

This spell is not directed at a particular person, so you
don't need to worry about getting permission. It is a way of
strengthening old friendships and encouraging new ones. After
you have cast this spell, plan to spend some time with each of
your friends, doing something that you both enjoy. The best
time to cast this spell is during the new moon—with a window
open through which you can see it.

You will need:

- Pen and paper
- Two teaspoons of almond
  oil mixed with one drop of
  patchouli essential oil
- White tea light candle

INCANTATION
Friends meet, friends greet,
Companions all, kind and sweet.
Strengthen ties and fill each heart,
True friends never will depart.

A SPELL TO GIVE POWER
TO A FRIENDSHIP

1. Rub a few drops of the mixed oil on the surface of the candle and on the inside of your wrists.

2. Carefully light the candle.

3. On one piece of paper, draw a picture of your face (this can be a few simple lines!), and write down three qualities that make you a good friend.

4. On another piece of paper, draw other faces, and write down three qualities that you like your friends to have.

5. Say the incantation as you put a drop of oil on one corner of each piece of paper.

6. Let the candle burn out.

FRIENDS REUNITED

Magic should never be used to force another person to act against their will. Therefore, you cannot cast a spell to make your friend apologize. However, you can cast a spell to smooth the way toward making up. This spell will help to clear the way, so that you can walk toward each other and meet in the middle. Cast this spell during a waxing moon. It is best performed outdoors, during daylight.

You will need:

- Apple, cut in two
- Piece of white paper, no bigger than the apple
- Pen
- Two cocktail sticks

A SPELL TO MAKE UP WITH A FRIEND

1. Write your full name and your friend's full name on the piece of paper.

2. Place the paper between the two halves of the apple.

3. Visualize your friendship being healed. Think about what went wrong and how it can be mended. Accept that you are responsible for the argument as well as your friend.

4. Insert a cocktail stick from right to left to pin the apple halves together, picturing yourself walking toward your friend with your hands held out toward them.

5. Insert the second cocktail stick from left to right, picturing your friend walking toward you with their hands held out toward you.

6. Send your love to your friend, and ask to receive their love in return. You can then take the apple apart and dispose of it.

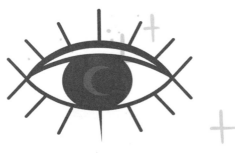

MAGIC UMBRELLA

This spell can help a friend at times when they are feeling vulnerable or sensitive. You can't protect them completely from the world around them, but you can keep the damage to a minimum, just like an umbrella! This spell works over the course of a day and a night. It is best performed at the time of a waxing moon.

You will need:

- Rose quartz pendant
- Long piece of ribbon

INCANTATION

Protection for you, from my heart to yours.
Faithful and true, on seas and on shores.
Wrap you in cotton, defend you from harm.
Never forgotten, I fill up this charm.

A SPELL TO PROTECT YOUR FRIEND

1. As soon as you wake up, thread the pendant onto the ribbon, and put it around your neck.

2. Three times during the day and three times after sunset, take out the pendant and hold it in both hands as you say the incantation. Then kiss the pendant, and put it back underneath your clothes.

3. Wear the pendant all night. In the morning, give the pendant to your friend and ask them to wear it under their clothes, close to their heart, whenever they feel they need your support.

4. Explain that it is for their protection, to show that you are thinking of them and care about them.

So Long, Sadness

This simple spell is intended to lighten the heart of your friend during a time of pain or worry. Make sure your friend knows that you are there to help and support them. If you listen to your friend's needs, you will always be able to support them. You should perform this spell before noon during the time of a new moon.

You will need:

- Piece of card
- Pen
- Brown candle
- Ylang-ylang incense
- Turquoise crystal
- Envelope

INCANTATION
Take away sadness, take away sorrow.
Bring my friend a new tomorrow.
Unseen powers, hear this plea;
Let [friend's name] happier be.

A SPELL TO CHEER UP A FRIEND

1. Light the candle and the incense, thinking about your friend and their state of mind.

2. Fold the card in half, and on the front, draw a figure eight. This represents endless friendship.

3. Pass the crystal through the incense smoke three times, saying the incantation.

4. Place the crystal in the middle of the figure eight. Visualize the worry and sadness leaving your friend and entering the crystal.

5. Snuff out the candle, then remove the crystal from the figure-eight and wash it under running water.

6. Write these words inside the card: Forever, Radiant,  Inseparable, Encouraging, Necessary, Defender, Supportive. Sign the card with love, place it in the envelope, and give it to your friend.

CRYSTAL HEALING

Healing spells are an important part of magic. Spells can heal the emotional injuries of your spiritual self, as well as speeding up physical recovery. If you are performing this spell to heal someone else, remember to first ask their permission. You will be sending out powerful energy, and it is important to treat it with respect. This spell should be cast under a new moon.

You will need:

- Blue candle for healing
- White candle for power
- Pink candle for love
- Rosemary incense
- Clear quartz crystal
- The name of the person to be healed written on a piece of paper

INCANTATION

Friend, be healed by this gift of power,
Growing stronger hour by hour.
Energy flow through every part,
May health and happiness fill your heart.

A SPELL TO HEAL A FRIEND

1. Place the candles in a row, with the white candle in the middle. Carefully light the incense and the candles.

2. Put the paper with the name on it by the white candle, and place the crystal on top of the paper.

3. Visualize your own energy combining with the unseen energies of the universe. Enjoy the aroma of the incense. Take a few deep breaths, and imagine your energy increasing with each breath.

4. When you feel ready, release your healing energy. Direct it through the crystal toward the person you wish to heal.

5. Speak the incantation, then snuff out the candles.

Spells for Luck

Silver Guardian

There are all kinds of occasions when you might wish to protect an object. Perhaps you are going on a trip and want to make sure that your suitcase doesn't get lost. Maybe you are lending one of your most precious possessions to someone. Whatever the reason, this spell will help keep an object safe from harm or theft. This spell will work best on a Monday, during a waxing moon.

You will need:

- Basil leaf
- Silver ribbon
- The object you wish to protect

INCANTATION
**Protected is this [object name] of mine,
Safe from danger for all time.**

A SPELL TO PROTECT AN OBJECT

1. Place the basil leaf inside the object, or rub the leaf gently over the object.

2. Rest your first and middle fingers on the object.

3. Visualize a bright purple light streaming from your fingers and circling the object three times.

4. Weave the ribbon around the object.

5. Say the incantation three times.

6. Remove the ribbon, and keep it in a safe place.

SAFE TRAVELS

This spell will protect you on a journey, no matter how long or short. (It could just be the walk to school!) However, for the spell to work well, you must stay alert and focused on your trip. If you meet with a situation that makes you nervous, be sensible, follow your instincts, and if necessary, change your route. Cast this spell at home, as close to your travel time as possible.

You will need:

- Four small, white candles
- Sandalwood essential oil
- Square of dark blue fabric
- White cord
- Pinch of basil
- Pinch of rosemary
- Pinch of sea salt
- Clear quartz crystal
- Silver coin

INCANTATION
**Let our lives protected be,
Over land or over sea.
May this charm our
health maintain,
Till we come back
home again.**

A SPELL TO PROTECT YOURSELF ON A TRIP

1. Run a bath and add the essential oil. Position the candles at the four corners of the bathtub.

2. Lie in the bath and visualize the journey, imagining yourself arriving safely at your destination.

3. When you feel rested, finish your bath and blow out the tea lights.

4. Place the basil, rosemary, salt, quartz, and coin on the square of fabric, and say the incantation.

5. Using the white cord, tie the cloth into a pouch, and keep it close to you throughout your trip.

6. Relight the four candles when you get home as a thank you for the safe journey.

Lock in the Luck

Almost any object can be a lucky charm, but it should be something that means a lot to you—a present from a friend, a pebble you found on the beach, or a beautiful feather. The energy that you put into your lucky charm will triple, and keeping it close to you will remind you that luck is something you can choose to draw upon. Perform this spell on any day between the new moon and the full moon.

You will need:

- Blue tea light candle
- Rose incense
- Mint leaves
- The object you wish to turn into a lucky charm

INCANTATION

I open my eyes to the chances around me.
Health and happiness, wealth and safety.
Energies flow and mingle here.
Let this [object name] attract good cheer.

A SPELL TO MAKE A LUCKY CHARM

1. Carefully light the candle and the incense.

2. Hold the object in your writing hand, and visualize energy moving into your body—up from the earth and down from the sky.

3. Imagine the energy moving to the palm of your writing hand and passing into the object.

4. Recite the incantation.

5. Gently rub the object with the mint leaves, and allow the candle to burn out.

Sunny Spells

You should avoid trying to influence the weather too often. Nature knows what it's doing, and as a spellcaster you should show it respect. However, for special occasions, there are some ways to ask for fine weather. Weather spells are difficult, and your request may not always be granted. Before you decide to do this spell, think carefully—is it really vital to have good weather? If it is, you should perform the spell in your spellcasting space a week before the date.

You will need:

- Gold candle
- Red jasper crystal
- Paper and pen

INCANTATION
**Fair winds blow and bright sun shines
On this special day of mine.
Remember me a week from today,
And send the rain clouds far away.**

A SPELL TO ENCOURAGE FINE WEATHER

1. Draw a small map of the area where you want the sun to shine. It does not need to be accurate or detailed!

2. Carefully light the candle, and move the map clockwise around it three times. Focus on the flame.

3. Say the incantation, folding the paper in half each time you speak a line.

4. Place the folded paper under the crystal in a place beneath your window, and snuff out the candle.

Opportunity Knocks

You are surrounded by chances and opportunities every day. The more attention you pay to them, the more they will appear. For this spell to be most successful, you should hold in your mind the kind of opportunities you want. Meditate on them before you cast the spell. Set your imagination free and let it soar! You should perform this spell in your home and renew it every new moon.

You will need:

- Bowl of earth
- Square of green fabric
- White ribbon
- Pen, paper, and scissors
- Cedar incense
- Dried chamomile
- Mint essential oil
- Honeysuckle essential oil

INCANTATION

Force of chance, please work for me,
Guide me to opportunity.
Part of nature, part of earth,
Let me win what I am worth.

A SPELL TO CREATE OPPORTUNITIES

1. On the paper, draw a four-leafed clover. This should be small—about the size of a postage stamp. On one side, write your name, and on the other, draw a picture of yourself (it doesn't matter how good the drawing is). Now cut this out.

2. Lay out the fabric, then place the picture and the chamomile in the middle. Add one drop of mint oil and one drop of honeysuckle oil.

3. Bring the corners toward the middle. Tie them together like a small bag with the ribbon.

4. Say the incantation. As you speak, run your fingers through the earth in the bowl.

5. Carefully light the incense, and pass the bag through the smoke for a few seconds.

6. Keep the bag in a safe place in your bedroom.

Lost and Found

Whatever you have lost, this is a simple and fast-working spell to help you find it again. It is important to remember that this is a spell to locate lost objects. It should never be used on people or anything living. This spell works best during a full moon.

You will need:

- Three small green candles
- One small gold candle
- Picture of what is lost or something that symbolizes it

INCANTATION
**Turn this object's fate around.
What is lost shall now be found.
Show me what I need to find,
Relieve the worry on my mind.**

A SPELL TO FIND A LOST OBJECT

1. Carefully light the green candles, reciting part one of the incantation as you light them. In between lighting each candle, turn on the spot, clockwise.

2. Place the gold candle closest to you, near the picture of what is lost.

3. Recite the second part of the incantation as you light the gold candle.

4. Wait for the candles to burn out, and then the spell will start to work.

Spells for Love

Enchanted Valentine

This is a spell that allows the spellcaster a brief peek into the future. You can only perform this spell once a year, on the evening of February 13. This is the eve of St. Valentine's Day, and it is a night that shimmers with powerful energies.

You will need:

- Three almonds
- Pen and paper
- Any item of white clothing (even a sock will do!)

INCANTATION

Almonds sweet and wholesome three,
Show me who my love will be.
Let me glimpse in all or part
Where the future guides my heart.

A SPELL TO DREAM OF YOUR TRUE LOVE

1. Open your window, and breathe in the night air deeply.

2. Imagine yourself breathing in energy and breathing out tiredness and sadness.

3. Hold the three almonds in your writing hand, and recite the incantation.

4. Place the almonds beneath your pillow, then put on the white item of clothing.

5. Focus only on yourself as you drift off to sleep.

STAND OUT FROM THE CROWD

This is an enchantment to draw others toward you in a positive way—it doesn't mean that you will always want to be noticed by the people you attract! For best results, you should perform this spell during a full moon.

You will need:

- Circle of pink fabric
- Yellow ribbon
- Petals from a flower that you love
- Small, red paper heart
- Bright coin

INCANTATION

Seven knots for open eyes.
Seven knots inducing smiles.
Seven knots to let them see.
Seven knots to noticed be.

A SPELL TO GET NOTICED

1. Place the fabric circle in front of you on the ground or on an empty table.

2. Keeping your eyes on the circle, think about the type of person that you want to attract.

3. One by one, put the petals, heart, and coin on the fabric.

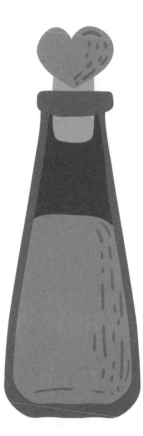

4. Tie the fabric into a pouch with the yellow ribbon, using seven knots. As you tie the knots, chant the incantation.

5. Hang the pouch beside your bed, so that it is close beside you when you dream.

SOUL SEARCHING

This is a spell that will draw a soul mate toward you. It is not to be cast on a particular person. Done well, it will attract love to you, but it won't work if you are upset or angry. Remember that happiness attracts happiness, love attracts love. The more loving you are toward your family, friends, and pets—even your plants!—the better this spell will work. Before you begin, use your meditation time to think about what love means to you and what a soul mate might be like.

INCANTATION
Love I give, and love I seek.
Bring to me a love unique.

You will need:

- Small box
- Red pen
- Vanilla incense
- Dried rosemary
- Rose quartz crystal
- Pink tea light candle

A SPELL TO MEET A SOUL MATE

1. Write "Love is mine" in red on the box.

2. Light the incense, then put the crystal and the rosemary in the box.

3. Put anything else that reminds you of love into the box, such as poems or heart-shaped candies. Don't put anything into the box that makes you think of a particular person.

4. Imagine yourself being happier than you've ever been.

5. Light the candle and say the incantation.

6. Snuff out the candle, then add it to the box.

7. Allow the incense to burn out, then shut the box.

You must not open the box again until you have met your soul mate. At that time, take the crystal out of the box and keep it safe. Bury the box in some earth.

Healing Hearts

Physical wounds heal quickly, but a broken heart can seem to last forever. No spell can completely heal it—only time and patience can do that. But this spell will help make it easier to bear. Above all, do not hold onto anger, jealousy, or bitterness. The happier you feel, the easier it is to forgive and let go of the past. You should perform this spell at home on a Friday morning or evening.

You will need:

- One herbal tea bag
- Sea salt
- Two pink candles
- Pink drawstring bag
- Rose quartz crystal
- Copper coin
- Small bowl
- A good pinch of dried strawberry leaves
- Three drops of strawberry oil

INCANTATION

Unseen powers, rise and flow,
Protect my heart, which sinks so low.
Help me through these heavy days,
Guide me to lighter, happier ways.

A SPELL TO EASE A BROKEN HEART

1. Make yourself a mug of herbal tea, and light one pink candle.

2. Run a bath, and pour some sea salt into it.

3. Take a bath while sipping the tea. When you're ready, get out of the bathtub, dry off, and get dressed.

4. Brush your hair, breathe deeply, and relax, then light the second pink candle.

5. In the bowl, mix together the strawberry leaves and strawberry oil. As you stir, look at yourself in the mirror while speaking the incantation.

6. Put half the mixture in the bag with the coin and crystal, and carry the bag with you.

7. Leave the other half of the mixture in the bowl, and keep it by your bed.

8. Repeat this spell every Friday for as long as you need to.

SEE THE FUTURE

For as long as anyone can remember, people have been trying to catch a glimpse of the future ... But at best, you can only hope to see a tiny flash. (Even then, you may not interpret it correctly!) So don't put all your trust in what you see. Instead, cast the spell with a happy, light heart, and have a little fun. You should perform this spell in your house, preferably before noon.

You will need:

- Square of blue fabric
- Ash leaves
- Bay leaves
- Holly leaves
- Jasmine petals
- Rose petals
- Marigold flowers
- Gold cord
- Pen and paper

INCANTATION
Sweetest sleep and inner sight,
Bless my magic dreams tonight.
Let me know what lies ahead,
While I slumber in my bed.

A SPELL TO PEEK INTO THE FUTURE

1. Lay out the fabric, then place the ash, bay, rose, holly, jasmine, and marigold in the middle.

2. Bring the corners toward the middle. Tie them with the cord to make a small pouch.

3. On the paper, write as clearly as you can what you wish to find out about the future.

4. Place the herbal bag and the note under your pillow, speaking the incantation.

5. Go straight to bed. Your dreams will bring you the answer to your question. As soon as you wake up, write the dream in your dream journal.

Spell Finder

"It is important to remember that we all have magic inside us."

J. K. ROWLING

Other titles in the series:
Astrology * Crystals * Palm Reading